What They Didn't Teach You About Recruiting

by Dan Tudor

Published by Embarcadero Group, Inc.   © 2014

What They Didn't Teach You About Recruiting

The website addresses cited in this text were current as of August 1, 2014, unless otherwise noted.

Tudor Collegiate Strategies
Embarcadero Group, Inc.
455 Kern St. Suite D
Shafter, California 93263

E-Mail the author, Dan Tudor, at dan@dantudor.com

Or, call Tudor Collegiate Strategies
866.944.6732

Table of Contents

Introduction

As you begin reading this book, chances are you're one of those coaches who don't know what they don't know.

You shouldn't feel guilty about that, by the way. You were never taught. You, like most coaches, jumped straight from your college student-athlete days right into coaching duties. And even if you came to coaching from the "real world" after college, very few came to coaching with extensive sales, marketing and communication experience.

This book, hopefully, will change that for you. I wanted this book to focus on all of the stuff that college athletic departments *should* teach their coaches, but never get around to doing. It deals with many of the subjects that they did not teach you before they asked you to go out and sell your program to a teenage athlete, and his or her parents. As you have started to do that, you have probably noticed that it is not as easy as you may have first thought - getting the attention of a recruit, starting a conversation, getting them to visit campus, and getting them to commit...all of it is much more challenging than anything your

4

sport could throw at you on the court, field, track or pool. *This book will help.*

This book features a collection of training tips and articles originally published at dantudor.com as a part of our weekly training sessions for college coaches (hopefully, you're familiar with them as a subscriber to our free College Recruiting Weekly Newsletter). I have put them together, and added additional tips, techniques, strategies and thoughts to them. You will find that much of the new material is based on my conversations with coaches like yourself over the years.

Each of these chapters features proven tips and techniques proven to make an immediate impact in your recruiting efforts. Some you will like, some you will likely question, but I am pretty sure each of them will make you think. You'll think about the way you do things now, the way you want to do things, and you'll get some ideas of how to change the way you recruit. I am hoping you are not only educated by what we talk about in this book, but also inspired and challenged as a serious college recruiter.

One last thing: This book was written at the prompting of coaches, mainly from our On-Campus training seminars that we conduct and from extended one-on-one sessions I have had the pleasure of having with our Premium Members and clients of our Total Recruiting Solution plan. So, I wanted to take this

opportunity to thank you all very, very much. I think I have learned as much from you as you have learned from me, and you have given me the chance to help you become better at what you do. That's been the most rewarding part of writing these books, and being asked to come alongside many of you and help you with your ongoing recruiting efforts.

If you have question, want to talk about getting better at recruiting, or sound off on a topic we discuss here, just e-mail me at dan@dantudor.com. I'd love to hear from you.

Let's get started.

6

<u>LESSON ONE</u>:

They Didn't Teach You That You *Always* Need to Take a Fresh Look at the Way You Recruit

There comes a point in every coach's year when they hit a wall.

They're tired of recruiting. Tired of the phone calls that are not being returned. Tired of the budget limits they have to stay within in trying to woo a recruit to their campus. Basically, they're facing "recruiting burn-out."

Maybe you're going through that phase right now. You're getting weary, you've run out of ideas, and you're tired of the same approaches that don't seem to work. As one coach told me recently, "Recruiting gets so frustrating sometimes, I feel like I just want to throw down the phone and walk out of the office."

Sound familiar? If it describes you, I want to give you a few ideas for shaking up your approach and maybe, *just maybe*, come up with some new ideas on how to recruit more effectively and creatively.

The concept I'm talking about comes courtesy of business and marketing author Edward de Bono, and its called "S.C.A.M.P.E.R."

That is an acronym for:

·**Substitute**

·**Combine**

·**Adapt**

·**Modify, Maximize or Minimize**

·**Put to other use**

·**Reverse or Rearrange**

In the business world, this is a great way to look at an old idea or process in a new way, then asking questions on how to improve it. The letters, and words that they represent, are parts of the creative process. Most businesses make it a regular practice to

8

constantly re-evaluate the way they do things, and what are the most effective methods for marketing to their potential customers or clients.

College coaches don't usually do that. But they need to.

So, how do you use this concept as a coach? Pick an area of your recruiting process - let's say, for example, the prospect letters that you send out to a prospect who you are making contact with for the very first time. Take a look at whatever letter or text that you use. The key here is to throw any idea out for consideration and write it down. Don't focus on the budget, or what your fellow coaches would say about it, or if it makes sense or not. Just brainstorm.

Now, let's apply the S.C.A.M.P.E.R. principal to it...*and focus on creativity.*

Substitute – What if you used something else besides a piece of white paper? Changed the font? Mailed it in something besides the standard #10 envelope? Put something else attention grabbing in it besides the standard brochure?

I recommend not looking like everyone else when it comes to mailing something to a prospect. Different is better, Coach.

Especially considering that your teenage audience is becoming more and more immune to our traditional ways of trying to communicating with them. They have not grown up using and relying on the mail as you and I probably have, so to be effective in this day and age you need to think of ways to be a more creative communicator. Is there anything you could substitute in your current mailings that would grab a recruit's attention more than you are now?

Since we're talking about traditional mail, let me make one thing clear: Our ongoing focus group research clearly indicates that there is a place for good old-fashioned mailed letters. If you think about that for a moment, it makes sense: They have grown up in a world where they haven't interacted with mail in the same way that we may have as adults. So, when they receive letters on a consistent basis from coaches, it makes an impact. Mail needs to be part of any good recruiting plan. (Just make sure that once they get your letter, and open it, that it doesn't sound like the same kind of boring message they've received from other coaches).

Combine - What if you combined the letter and the envelope into one piece? Or how about including your business card with your form letter? Better yet, what if you designed a special web address with a special message for new prospects and "combine"

10

it with your letter by pointing your new prospect to it when they read the letter? Again, the key here is to be creative with some of the older, more traditional methods of recruiting communication (you know, the stuff that a lot of college coaches have given up on). Look for different ways to present your information to your recruit in a way that combines two old, tired methods that you're using right now into a new, creative idea to use with your prospects. So, can you combine things together into something new and fresh?

Adapt - Can your message be better adapted to fit all of the new media options available to recruits? Is there a way to reach new prospects through more creative mailings? Through an inexpensively produced online video? How about posting videos of your team and your program on YouTube, Facebook and other social media outlets? Do you have a dedicated social media page for your team, and for you as a coach? Could you put your message to new prospects on a blog? (Do you have a blog? Do you know what a blog is? Have you reserved your own name as an internet domain name?) Be creative - adapt your traditional recruiting message to new media that will get the response from today's teen (and their parents, who increasingly use social media and the Internet to evaluate and interact with potential college coaches for their son or daughter's athletic future).

Modify, Maximize or Minimize - What can you enlarge, shrink or alter about your traditional recruiting mailing? What if you made your personal business card post card sized? What if it were extra small, or a different shape? Be creative...think of ways to modify, maximize or minimize your mailings.

The reason this can be powerful really just comes down to the simple idea that different is better. For student-athletes who are getting significant contact from a variety of different programs, sometimes being different is the thing that an athlete will gravitate to as they pick the college (and coach) to take seriously based on how different they are from the rest of the pack. In the research that we do for our clients and in the campus workshops we lead, your current student-athletes tell us that the coach who looked, sounded or acted different made a significant impact on them as they began to assign value to particular programs. In short, *"different works"*.

Put to other use - Do you have materials lying around that you could use in your mailing to a new class of recruits? Think out of the box. Maybe you're a baseball or softball coach...what if you included some dirt from your diamond in a little plastic zip-lock bag to help get your prospect excited about playing on your field? Be creative: Look at some of the ordinary things that you

12

have all around you that a high school hopeful might get excited about, and use it in your initial mailing.

What you're trying to do, of course, is "connect" with your prospect. And I have to be honest, Coach: There aren't a lot of traditional college brochures out there that connect with teenagers (including yours).

Reverse or Rearrange - In your process of contacting new recruits, what would happen if you reversed the order you did things? Or, if you rearranged what happens in the process? Be creative...shake up the status quo by reversing or rearranging your process for how you approach new prospects. For instance, one coach I know starts out recruiting every one of her prospects with a phone call. She lets them know that she's interested in them, and what they'll be receiving in the coming weeks that will tell them more about her program. Of course, different NCAA rules will determine if that kind of a "reversal" would work for you. But the point is she sets herself apart from her competition by reversing the traditional order of things. And it works. Why? Because it is different.

Those were just a few brief examples of how you might use the S.C.A.M.P.E.R. method to creatively approach what most coaches describe as a mundane part of their job: Prospect communication. But just think about how many other facets of

13

your recruiting operation that you can take a fresh look at using this creative, proven approach: Phone calls, e-mails, personal visits...and, yes, even those recruiting letters that tend to be the first thing you're tempted to ditch because of how old and tired they may sound to you.

To win in your sport, you and your staff are constantly assessing your team's talent and building a game plan around that talent. To recruit and sign the best talent, you need to do the same thing with your recruiting materials and your staff's process of recruiting the athletes you need. If you do what everybody else is doing, you won't set yourself apart. And that makes recruiting all the more difficult when you're dealing with a generation of student-athlete prospect that is craving - and demanding - a consistent, original approach to communicating with them.

One of the best examples of taking a fresh approach to how he recruits every day is a coach in SEC-country who oversees recruiting for a small school football program. Now I don't know about you, but recruiting in the same state as some of college football's traditional power programs doesn't seem like it should be "easy".

But this coach takes a creative approach. He's not under the same kind of tight regulations that shackle his larger D1 counterparts, and he takes advantage of it. His mailings are cool
14

and creative. He writes his own online blog (be alarmed if you do not know what a blog is, coach) and consistently links it back to his personal and team social media sites. He uses video, instant messaging and other forms of communicating, but he always tries to put a unique twist on it. And, he always tries to be first with the earliest possible communication. In short, he never does something that doesn't "push the envelope" a little. He is always taking chances, and always trying to look at different ways to "SCAMPER" his message to his prospects – who, by the way, are paying attention to his message.

So, get "SCAMPERing", Coach! Look for ways to change, evolve, and put a fresh spin on the way you recruit and communication with your prospects.

<u>LESSON TWO</u>:

They Didn't Teach You How to Rekindle a Prospect's Interest in Your Program

Remember those recruits that you were really interested in pursuing earlier in the year, but then for one reason or another they just fell off the radar?

They're probably still out there, Coach. You may have been waiting for them to contact you, but they didn't. Or they thought you were going to be calling them, but you didn't. And now both you sit, waiting for the other person to make the first move in rekindling the interest in playing at your college.

The fact that those types of prospects, whom you've already made some sort of contact with, are still out there and are quite possibly representing a huge potential recruiting resource for you. It's smart to try and go after this group of athletes for a few proven reasons:

16

- They're probably already familiar with you as a coach, a program, and the overall basics of what you could offer them in terms of a scholarship or playing opportunity.

- They're still interested in playing college sports somewhere (assuming they haven't already committed to a competitor).

- They're probably feeling a little anxious about their plans for after high school, especially if they're an upperclassman and are now considered "late" to commit in their sport compared to some of their top-tier peers.

So, what's the best way to go after this group, get their attention again, and rekindle the communication and their interest in your program?

Here are a few proven ideas on how to approach this group of prospects, based on our experience in working with coaching staffs on a client basis over the past few years:

Apologize for the lack of communication. Sure, it is probably partly (or mostly) their fault for not communicating. But as the person who is initiating the contact, and as the "authority figure" in the relationship, you need to be the one to apologize. It will take the pressure off of them and open the door for ongoing communication. You want to make it easy for them to start communicating with you

17

again, and we've seen that when a coach takes the blame for letting the communication falter.

Look for ways to take the blame. Doing so significantly increases the likelihood that they will be able to pick-up where they left off with those recruits. It also communicates that there isn't any lingering awkwardness or hurt feelings on your part, which is important for this generation of student-athlete since many are less equipped than previous generations at communicating with adults when it comes to resolving potential misunderstandings.

Call with LOTS of urgency. Be honest with them that you're looking to wrap up your recruiting efforts by a certain point (maybe 30 or 60 days out). Tell them that you've been waiting to hear back from them, but haven't, so you wanted to be a little forward and push the process ahead to the next step. Tell them that at this point you see them as a high priority recruit who can make an impact in your program, but you need a final answer soon as to whether they are interested in pursuing a spot on your team. I worked with a college volleyball coach who is one of our Premium Members and we used this approach with a great prospect that was looking at twelve different schools, including his school. Since our coach was the only one that had called her with urgency and firmly "asked for the sale",

18

she went with him. The coach said that his prospect has since told him that none of the other coaches went this far in urgently asking her for a commitment, and that she liked the fact that he really fought to get her to come to his school.

Call with the assumption that they've signed with someone else, and offer your congratulations. If they have signed with another school, you'll come off as a class act. Make sure you take the time to ask two or three questions about why your prospect chooses the other school - that will come in handy the next time you are selling against them. If they haven't signed with another school, they'll tell you. And, the door will be re-opened! You'll still look like a class act, and you can re-kindle your recruiting conversation again. If you do have the opportunity to talk with the prospect again about scholarship possibilities, make sure you use one of the techniques I listed above to get the process rolling again quickly. <u>Remember, you now have a valuable second chance with this athlete</u>. Take full advantage of it.

Wouldn't it be great if talented prospects were the one's calling *you* consistently? Sure it would. But it's usually not in the teen's personality make-up to take that kind of initiative and boldly call a college coach. It's just too intimidating.

You have to be the one to rekindle the relationship.

19

This is a big, untapped pool of prospects for most coaches, and many of these kids are more apt to be responsive now that time has passed and their window of opportunity to play college sports is getting smaller and smaller.

Will you take advantage of it?

<u>LESSON THREE</u>:

They Didn't Teach You How to "Super Size" Your Coaching Networking Opportunities

It is amazing what a business sales professional or business owner can do at a trade show or networking event that he or she cannot manage to do from 9 to 5 during a normal workday.

At trade shows, local Chamber of Commerce events, conventions and other gatherings of business professionals, savvy sales and marketing representatives can make contacts, exchange contact information and bend the ear of some very important decision makers in their area - people who wouldn't otherwise have the time for them during a normal business day.

What have these talented, successful sales professionals learned over their careers that many college coaches still struggle with?

It's simple:

Networking with the right people and companies open doors and create opportunities. The <u>same</u> principles hold true for a college coach.

Actually, you might be able to identify with some good networking practices when you go to a national coaches convention for your sport. Both by nature and by design, you probably spend time talking with your fellow coaches. You want to keep your name out there – just in case. If you're a head coach, you never know when you'll be looking for another assistant, and it's a lot easier to snag a good one if they already know you, and you know them. If you're an assistant looking for bigger and better opportunities, there's no better place than a convention to press some flesh, make new contacts, and expand your network. After all, assistants never know when they're going to be looking for that next job, and it's a lot easier to snag a good one if a head coach already knows you, and you know them.

Networking in your day to day coaching life isn't hard, really. But it does take organization and a little bit of time (the later of the two is the reason why many college coaches struggle with it). And, once that time is devoted to the project, coaches usually see the payoff pretty quickly.

The same proven principles of networking can play a part in putting together future classes of really good prospects, too. I wanted to give you three easy ways to "super size" your recruiting network without adding a lot of time to your day, or subtracting a lot of money from your already tight budget. Here they are:

1. **Call a high school or club coach.** I can hear it now..."Come on, Dan! I already have a list of high school coaches I send stuff to!" Read the tip again. I didn't say "send more stuff to them", I said to *call* them. Most of your competition sends "stuff" to high school and club coaches. So why be like everyone else? Generalized mass mail gets minimal attention from anyone, especially busy high school and club coaches, which you've probably noticed to some extent. Asking them to fill out a form - whether it's on paper or online - with their top prospects doesn't get a huge return on your investment, right? Phone calls to a coach will have the best chance of changing that, from what my staff and I have noticed in the past few years of working closely with college coaches. Call one new coach every day in the office. Ask them who they have that's good in the current class you're focused on and in the next two classes you'll be recruiting. Ask them who they'd recommend from another team. Ask them if they need advice

23

on anything related to recruiting, or any instructional tips that have worked for you. Spend just ten minutes talking to them, and you will have taken a big step towards creating a recruiting disciple ready to spread the word about your program to their kids. I've seen it happen, and it works. Just think: If you did that every day, for just ten minutes a day, you'd build your network to over 200 coaches in just one year, and have those coaches be enthusiastic about your program because you took a few minutes to introduce yourself to them.

2. **Give a half hour talk out-of-town**. You're there recruiting a kid anyway, right? Why not make the most of it and make your athlete feel special in the process? Develop a basic, short 30-minute talk on recruiting, giving the local sports community some good advice on what colleges look for and some important tips on going through the process (by the way, that's another great way to earn a connection with a local high school or club coaches). Become the perceived expert when it comes to your sport and recruiting just by giving away some information that every parent and athlete needs, without asking for anything in return. Worried about athletes using your info and signing with the competition? It won't be because of your talk. In fact, your newly acquired "expert status" is going to earn you points and sway people to your

program and your college. Use your time in a community to give away some good advice and make good networking contacts. It's the best use of your time when you're on the road!

3. **Get recruiting contacts for other coaches in your department**. Stick with me on this one: When you're talking with a prospect you're recruiting out of your area, why not ask them who the other stand-out athletes at their school are in sports besides your won? Who are the up-and-coming underclassmen? Who are the better athletes that you could pass on to other coaches in your department? You'll be surprised how many names of good athletes you'll collect. Then, go back to your college and play Santa Claus, handing out all of these leads to your fellow coaches throughout the department. Do it over, and over, and over again. You know what will happen next? The other coaches in your department will start doing the same for you. And you'll get some good tips on athletes that you would have otherwise never known about.

The secret to successful networking is to <u>have a plan</u>, and then to <u>execute that plan</u>.

25

Every time I attend a coach's convention or go to a school to train a coaching staff, I take time to focus on developing relationships that will grow in the months and years to come.

Going to a convention or trade show to execute a plan is more work than going there to goof-off and have a good time, I realize. But I'm there to build my organization and my contact level with coaches and athletic directors.

In the same way, you need to view your recruiting trips or dead times in the office as golden opportunities to build your network of contacts who can (and will) act as unofficial "sales reps" for your program with their athletes. High school coaches love to drop names of a college coach that called them, and will return the favor by recommending good prospects to you, and recommending *you* to their student-athletes.

That's the ultimate definition of a "win-win" situation, and you can thank your investment of time in "super sizing" your network relationships for it.

26

LESSON FOUR:

They Didn't Teach You How to Ask Your Prospect Questions That Make Them Stop and Think

You wouldn't think that how you ask a question would be so important in determining how well you do in recruiting. But it does, Coach.

How you ask your prospect questions determines how well, and how quickly, you and your prospect connect. And that will probably determine whether or not they come to visit campus, commit to you, and join your program. And that sequence of events will probably determine whether or not you will be reaching for the Extra Strength Tylenol and regrouping with your coaching staff as you see your recruiting dreams go up in smoke, or looking forward to a championship season next year.

For example, one of our Total Recruiting Solution clients, who is a D1 women's soccer coach, began working with us after he had two recruits that he was *sure* were coming to his school call him within a week's time of each other and tell the coach that they were going elsewhere. Just like hundreds of other programs around the country, both large and small, this soccer coach is faced with a problem midway through his recruiting year: He needs to get his recruiting efforts back on track. **And fast**.

If you have read one of my other books, *"Selling for Coaches"*, you know the importance we place on asking the right questions at the right time. It's what determines how well coaches connect with athletes, and how likely it is that they will move to the point of being ready to commit to your program.

There are two types of questions that most coaches need to ask:

Questions that are asked to **get information and facts** from their prospect, and questions that are asked to **get insight on how or when their decision will be made**.

Both are essential to a college recruiter, who needs the answers if they are going to successfully move that prospect towards a decision to sign with their program.

With that in mind, here are two fantastic types of questions to ask your prospects that will get them to stop and think, and (more importantly) seriously look at your program. We've found that coaches can easily use them to get their recruiting efforts back on

28

track, and get better connected with the athletes they're still recruiting.

Change the way you ask an informational question. Instead of asking a prospect "So why are you interested in our program?" you might ask them "If you had to pay us for the right to play in our stadium, what would be your reason for doing that?"

Alternatively, instead of asking a prospect "Do you need any financial aid?" perhaps you should ask them "What kind of help could we give you on the financial side of things to make us a serious consideration in your mind?"

Notice the difference in how you're asking the same basic question? The second type of questioning style makes the prospect stop in his or her tracks and think. Why? Because if you ask a question like this, it forces them to let their guard down and expose what they're really thinking. It's not the typical way to ask a prospect a question, which will probably catch them off-guard a little bit. That's a good thing, coach. Getting them to really stop and think, and then listening carefully to how they answer the question, will give you the chance to connect with them in a way that most of your competition will miss out on.

Change the way you ask a timeline question. I've heard a lot of coaches ask a prospect they really want, "So when do you think you'll be making your final decision?" Or, they won't ask

29

any kind of decision-making question, opting instead to not appear "pushy" and just give the prospect some space.

Instead, what if you asked them, "Run me through how you're going to be making your decision, and who all is involved in helping you decide?" After they tell you the first part of their answer and stop (which they always do), you should ask, "And then what?" They'll tell you a little more, and you ask "And then what." And so it goes until you really get down to the nitty-gritty details of how the decision is really going to be made, and who is helping them make that decision. I can't emphasize enough the importance of asking *"And then what?"* at least three or four times in the same conversation with a prospect. It won't be until your third or fourth *"And then what"* that you really uncover how your prospect's decision will be made, who will be helping them make it, and when it will be made.

One other important aspect to these types of questions is that they need to be written out ahead of time. It's difficult, if not impossible, to ask these questions on the fly.

Here's the trouble with waiting until the phone call or personal visit to think of those questions: *It's really hard to do while actively thinking at the same time.* And sometimes, the questions you think of at the spur of the moment don't come out so good. So make sure you write out a few thought-provoking questions

30

ahead of time, commit them to memory, and determine what you're looking for in whatever their answer is.

Your questions are important - *vitally important* - to the whole process. The biggest benefit to asking fantastic and original questions (other than staying organized, controlling the sales process, and making your calls and conversations more productive and insightful) is that you'll sound smarter and more interested in your prospect compared to other coaches who ask the same "yes, no" boring questions that recruits have heard before. In fact, that might be the biggest benefit of all.

It all comes down to the questions you ask, and how you use those questions to quietly but consistently sell yourself and your program to the prospect you really, really want.

<u>LESSON FIVE</u>:

They Didn't Teach You How to Maximize Your E-Mail When You're Recruiting

I communicate with coaches by e-mail a lot. And many times, I'll get an automatic reply like this one from a coach I tried to e-mail:

"I am out of the office until January 5th. I won't be checking me e-mail. If you need immediate assistance, contact the athletic office at…"

Sound familiar? It should.

Chances are good that this type of automated e-mail response is a part of *your* normal e-mail routine when you're out of the office. Actually, coach, I know that it is…over a recent winter break, many of your e-mail servers sent back automatic e-mail replies when the College Recruiting Weekly Newsletter you subscribe to hit your Inbox.

Now on the one hand, it is good for someone like me or one of your prospects to know that you are not in your office. That

32

gives us a piece of valuable information – mainly, that we won't be hearing anything from you for the next several days.

But let's think about this for a second. Is that kind of response "good for business"? What I should ask is, *"Will that kind of automated e-mail reply help you reinforce the positive message about your program that you're hoping will stick with your prospects?"* The answer, obviously, is no.

Automated e-mail responses are a great concept – if they are done properly. One of the things we stress when we're advising clients about their email messages is that any e-mail communication is an opportunity to reinforce your brand and sell your program to that prospect. **EVERY time, EVERY e-mail.**

The automated email reply scenario I just outlined is just one of the shortfalls we've uncovered over the years in working with college coaches. It's important that recognizing the mistakes that you, as well as your competition, may be making when you type out those pre-vacation e-mails on your office computer may ruin the chances of forming a good initial relationship with your prospect.

To aid you in recognizing where you may be making mistakes in your email communication with recruits, here are four e-mail disasters we see happening from today's college coaches when it comes to automated responses that they send back to someone that contacts them when they're out of the office. See if you're in danger of any of these communications no-no's:

No creative, enthusiastic greeting. College coaches are some of the most positive people I know when it comes to singing the praises of their college, and their program when they're on the phone or seeing someone in person. However, when it comes to e-mail, many coaches like to keep it overly business-like and boring when they are typing out a greeting. And they do so to their own detriment.

Do you have a dull, uninteresting greeting in your e-mail auto-responder? Take a few minutes to think about a more upbeat, energetic greeting that one of your prospects might read. Focus on action-oriented, present-tense, energetic words and phrases that will engage your teenage prospect.

Telling readers what you *won't* do for them. "I won't be checking e-mail." Or, "I won't be checking my voicemail." Negative statements send the wrong message to a very important audience: Your recruits, their parents or their coaches. Choose positive alternatives to those statements that get the same message across.

Tell them what you *will* do while you're out of the office. You *will* have another coach follow-up with them. You *will* get back with them once you return back to town. You promise that you *will* follow-up with a phone call by a certain date once you get back. Notice the difference in the tone?

Positive, coach. Keep it positive, and emphasize what you will do for these prized prospects who contact you while you're out of the office!

Assuming that the sender's e-mail is unimportant. Many coaches will state that if the reader needs immediate help, here is who to contact. Then, coaches leave instructions to call the general receptionist, or give an alternative e-mail address to a coach that is covering for them.

You may not intend it to be, but the wrong language in your e-mail reply can give that "unwanted" impression. Every e-mail from a prospect is gold. You may not get another chance to hear from them, and they may go away feeling like you're not a coach who is really interested in hearing from them, or worse: They may come away with the feeling that you're probably not interested in them and that they are bothering you.

Make sure they come away with a clear, crisp picture in their mind that they are VERY important, and that it's imperative they know that you'll be in touch with them when you return. And, if you have a coach covering your e-mails for you as we suggested in the last point (and you should), make sure they send a quick reply offering themselves as a contact.

Not giving them "something to chew on". Once you've engaged them in a creative opening, giving them a positive statement about what you will do for them, and making sure they know they're important and valued, you need to give them a fact they didn't know about your program: Your latest win, a big recruiting class that you just officially signed, a move up in the rankings, a coaching honor or award that you've won...something that will give them another reason to want to talk to you (or *keep* talking to you).

Well written, interesting facts create talking points for your prospect and keep you on the mind of your recruit.

36

Does all of this take longer? Yes. More hassle? Without a doubt. Does it pay dividends by making you stand out from the crowd even while you are on the golf course or on vacation? Absolutely!

Don't pick this vital form of communication as the time when you're going to quit paying attention to details. E-mail and text messages are THE preferred methods of communication by today's teens. Even in this age of rampant social media use by this generation of recruits, email still rules when it comes to both early stage and ongoing recruiting contact (the research proves that pretty conclusively). NCAA rules allow some coaches in certain division levels to use text messaging to communicate with prospects, but the point is you should understand *how* your prospects prefer to communicate and try to use as many of those communication methods as possible. If you don't play by their rules, you'll end up paying the price.

Now, what about normal e-mail communication with your prospects? There are some rules to follow in this area, as well.

E-mail communication between college coaches and the athletes they recruit is at an all-time high, according to the NCAA, and as I just mentioned it is the preferred method of initial communication between coaches and the prospects they are recruiting (in addition to instant messaging and text messaging, if you are coaching in a division where that is allowed).

With e-mail, the whole concept is built around "read it when it's convenient for you". Your prospect picks up your e-mail message two days after you sent it? No big deal, that happens all the time, and there are no negative connotations with that.

So, when it comes to using e-mail to communicate with athletic prospects, the big question is this: *How can you effectively recruit using e-mail?* I'll give you five tips that I guarantee will improve your e-mail response from your prospects that you're recruiting.

Pay attention to the subject line in your e-mail! It's an afterthought for many coaches, but the subject line will make you or break you when it comes to getting your e-mail read. What makes an effective subject line? Asking a compelling question is best, I find.

For instance: "Have you seen what we offer our recruits?" Or, "Do you think you're good enough to crack our starting line-up?" Or, "Five reasons most athletes BEG us to recruit them." Maybe your subject lines are already provocative and compelling. Or,

38

maybe they're not. You be the judge, but I'll tell you this: I've seen colleges we have consulted with in-depth do the next four recommendations we're going to give you but ignore the subject line, and doing so has crippled some campaigns. The subject line is one of the most important aspects of your e-mail strategy, put a lot of thought into it (if you're a client of Tudor Collegiate Strategies, contact us so that we can help you create great subject lines for any email that you need to send out).

Keep it short. The shorter, the better. Why? First, teenagers have an incredibly short attention span. Most of them aren't interested in a lot of details, at least not in one large e-mail message. That's why most of your recruiting letters you send via mail have little or no real impact on most of your prospects (sorry, coach, but it's the truth).

Short e-mails get read, long ones get "scanned". You know what the difference is, because you do the same thing when you receive a lengthy e-mail...you "scan" it quickly, and then either re-read it or delete it. Short e-mails should be simple and to the point, especially if its in the beginning of the recruiting process. Shorter e-mails create a natural curiosity for the reader, and they will want to seek out more information in most cases.

Keep the core message very simple. That goes along with the first point, but there's a very specific purpose for simplicity in a recruiting e-mail: Comprehension. Would you rather rattle-off fifteen facts and figures about your program to a new recruit, or would it make more sense to give them an ongoing series of bite-sized chunks that they could read, absorb, understand and tie-in with the last easy-to-read bite-sized chunk that they got from you? The answer should be pretty obvious.

Remember who your audience is. They're being bombarded with information, images and choices on an almost hourly basis, day in and day out. They probably won't nibble on complex introductory messages, but they'll gobble down bite-sized chunks. Keep your messages simple, especially at the start of your communication with an athlete.

Don't beat around the bush. Get to the point when it comes to why you're contacting them. Do so while keeping your message short and keeping it simple. Don't get wrapped up in your amazing grasp of the English language...no flowery introductions, no ultra-formal paragraphs that eventually lead to why you're contacting them. Let them know - as soon as possible - what your interest is, why they should care about that interest, and what your interest could mean for them personally. That is the key to connecting with your prospect better than your competitor, a subject we explore in-depth in our first book for recruiters, *"Selling for Coaches"*.

Another point I want to stress here: *The more interesting and thought-provoking your first sentence, the more likely the rest of your message will be read.* Ask them a question, state a surprising fact, or make a bold claim. Whatever it is, grab their attention in that first sentence so that they're inclined to read the rest of your e-mail message (and future e-mail messages, as well!)

E-mail is great because it is low cost, and is a preferred communication method by most athletes (especially if they don't want you to invade their social media world). But, you have to play by *their* rules and live in *their* world for that recruiting communication to be effective.

<u>LESSON SIX</u>:

They Didn't Teach You Why Logic Doesn't Always Work With Your Recruits

One of our clients was a little frustrated when I spoke to him over the phone recently.

For the second time that particular month, he had a prospect who was telling him that despite all that his program had to offer, the prospect was probably going to commit to someone else. What the coach couldn't figure out was <u>why</u>: His program offered more money, a better facility, and a top notch education. Logically, it was the perfect fit for the recruit. It was, in fact, an all-around better offer on paper.

Here's the problem:

Logic doesn't always work with your recruits.

So how did another coach steal away the prospect? Simple: He was probably able to hit on some strong emotion or need that the prospect had, and connected on those points better than his competitors. That coach was somehow able to find something

42

that he knew the prospect needed emotionally, and built his case around that need. For our coach, using all of the logic in the world wasn't going to help. For this prospect - and many, many others - logic will almost <u>never</u> beat out emotional need. If you've been recruiting for any length of time now, you know that you don't need to be Einstein to figure that fact out.

Therefore, smart coaches will want to focus on meeting that need through their recruiting efforts every single time. They need to assume that their prospect's emotions will play a part (probably a *big* part!) in their final decision.

Wait, I can hear the objections already: *"Isn't that a lot like manipulating a prospect, Dan?"*

No.

Think about it, Coach. You're not "tricking" your prospect into doing something he doesn't want to do. Instead, when you approach recruiting correctly and intelligently, you're fulfilling a need he already has. You're building on an emotional need that he or she already has, and helping them figure out how to make themselves happy...how to meet their goals...and, quite literally, how to make their dream of playing college sports come true. It solves a problem that is worrying them...mainly, the problem of figuring out where would be the best place to continue their athletic career.

But hold on, coach! Before you start recruiting solely on emotion, here's the twist: If you do it, you'll fail almost as much as you would have if you keep using logic as your primary sales tool. Why? **Because people rarely make their final decisions based *solely* on emotion.** Research shows that doing so makes them feel guilty.

They may buy largely due to emotional needs, <u>but they also feel that they need good, solid facts to back up that emotional decision</u>. That helps them justify their choice, and makes them feel like they based their decision primarily on logic and facts.

Here's an example of what I'm talking about: You go out to buy a new iPhone. You buy it because you see your athletes use the latest version, and they're starting to make fun of you for using your old, out-of-date smart phone. Hey, if they think it's cool, it's gotta be worth it, right? Nothing wrong with that at all, coach. But that's an **emotional** reason to buy.

What happens when one of your fellow coaches asks you about it? You talk to them about staying up on the latest technology. How it lets you stream video, or take notes on your prospect when you're talking to them on the phone, or use apps that make

44

you more efficient at your job. Plus, they offered you a great data and minutes package, and it's going to save you $30 a month. Those are the **logical** reasons you buy.

It works the same way with your prospect, Coach. You need to connect with that emotional need to convince your prospect to "buy" what you're selling. But, at the same time, you need to give them the logical reasons to commit to your program. That way, when someone asks them why they chose you, they can say "I chose that program because..." and then cite reasons that make them look smart for making the decision they did.

Here's the bottom line: *There has to be a "because".*

Remember, making an emotionally based decision will probably make them feel guilty, or unintelligent. That's hard for our brains to work around, so we desperately search for logic and facts that will support our decision we want to make based on emotion. They need some good, solid logical reasons to back-up that decision that they just made.

Dr. Susan Weinschenk, writing for Psychology Today, makes the following observation about the principle of using the word "because" in an effort to make your point or gain agreement with someone else:

Using the word "because" and giving a reason resulted in significantly more compliance. This was true even when the reason was not very compelling ("because I have to make copies"). The researchers hypothesize that people go on "automatic" behavior or "mindlessness" as a form of a heuristic, or short-cut. And hearing the word "because" followed by a reason (no matter how lame the reason is), causes us to comply.

So what does this all mean?:

When the stakes are low people will engage in automatic behavior. If your request is small then follow the request with the word "because" and give any reason.

If the stakes are high, then there is a little more resistance, but still not too much. Use the word "because" and try to come up with at least a slightly more compelling reason.

Its a delicate mix, coach. And I'm not going to lie to you: It's not easy to balance the two. But there *has* to be that mix to successfully recruit an athlete. Too often, coaches use either logic or emotion. Not enough use both.

Make sure you're one of the savvy recruiters who successfully mixes both important aspects of connecting with a prospect.

Make sure you know what your "because" is when you're talking to a prospect so that you can appeal to their emotional – as well as their logical – decision making.

<u>LESSON SEVEN</u>:

They Didn't Teach You How to Negotiate With Your Prospects (and Their Parents)

When you want an athlete to commit - and he or she *wants* to commit to you and your program - it might seem like nothing can stand in your way. It's a done deal, right?

Not necessarily, as you probably know by now.

Maybe its pride, maybe its their parents...sometimes, your recruit might feel like they're "not getting what they deserve" and you have to sit down and iron out an agreement. Sometimes, signing an athlete comes down to some good old-fashioned hard ball negotiations. And, when it comes down to that, you need to make sure that you're in the best position possible to put together the kind of deal that works best for you and your program, while making the athlete feel like they are valued and important.

48

Is negotiating something coaches want to do, or like to do? Definitely not. But there are times when you'll be forced to roll up your sleeves and iron out differences that you have with a prospect, and doing it correctly and professionally will help to lay out the relationship you'll have with them for years to come.

Let me be clear about one thing here: *You need to be careful how, when and why you choose to employ these techniques.* Don't use them to manipulate your prospect; rather, *use them to stress your point of view in an effort to come to an agreement.* Don't use them to confuse your prospect; rather, use them to help them see your side clearly.

Negotiations are all about both sides getting what they want out of an agreement. In my opinion, there's nothing wrong with a coach getting the things he or she wants out of a scholarship deal, especially if that coach uses ethical, reasonable negotiating techniques in the process.

So, what's the key to a mutually beneficial negotiating process? Here are **four key negotiating techniques** that you can use next time you're locked in battle with a recruit and their parents over the terms of a scholarship offer you're making.

Learn to be shocked. "You want how much in books and tuition???" "You think you should be the starting center fielder

49

how soon??? Shock. Surprise. Visible flinching. *All* of these things make an immediate impact on the other person. And, unless they are a savvy sales and recruiting expert, they will either immediately become uncomfortable and try to rationalize their line of thinking to you, or they will concede some key points to you right away in the conversation.

Now I know that some coaches will object to this type of "acting" as a part of what they view as a normal conversation or typical back-and-forth in both parties coming to an agreement that they can live with. But here's what I want those coaches to understand: Several times, I have heard parents take great pride in being able to negotiate more out of a coach than they were first willing to give because of that kind of "acting". So, if many of your parents are going into a meeting with that mindset, wouldn't it be valuable for you as a recruiter to learn the same skills and be ready to use that skill if needed? I think it makes sense to do so.

As for acting shocked? It works, coach. Keep it in mind the next time you find yourself backed into a corner.

They ask, but will they receive? A lot of people - your teenage prospects and their parents included - will ask for a lot more than they expect to receive. And, they'll try to make you think that they other guys are offering more than they actually are. Keep this fact in mind, and avoid the temptation to immediately "price

50

match" to stay in the game. That doesn't mean that you never equal an offer made by a competitor if it is within your means to do it, but do so once you let the prospect explain how that point would be a key factor in them taking a closer look at your program and your offer. Ask them, for example, "Now that you've told me what State University is offering you, help me understand how matching that offer will make you more likely to sign with us?" What you're doing here is getting them to make a mental commitment to your program in offering up a reason why they will be more likely to commit to you if you're able to equal whatever one of your competitors has offered.

This is important, and will help you qualify them as a serious prospect and also establish your offer as better than your competitor's in the mind of your prospect and their parents.

If you have the most information, you'll win. Know your competitors inside and out. Ask the right questions to understand your prospect's situation and decision motives. To get good information, ask open-ended probing questions such as:

Who else have you been talking to?

What was your experience with that other coach when they spoke with you?

When will you be making your decision?

Only after you ask several open-ended, thought-provoking questions will you be able to assess the situation intelligently and know how to successfully lead your prospect down the path of signing with your program

Maintain your power of walking away. That's tough for a lot of coaches, and in some instances it isn't recommended. But if we're talking about an athlete that is abusing his relationship with you and your staff - taking too much of your time, demanding too much, parents are making unrealistic requests...you know who I'm talking about, coach - then its your right to walk away, and that's a very powerful negotiating tool. It's the same basic concept that many coaches use in offering a scholarship to a prospect, but giving them a deadline for accepting the offer. Basically, you're telling them that you will "walk away" if they don't commit.

If your prospect knows that you will move on to another recruit without hesitation, you'll maintain your control of the process and your position as the power player in the negotiating process. And can I tell you something else? You'll actually build respect in the process...your prospect could end up liking the fact that you're taking a strong position. People are drawn to strength, and it will often command more respect than groveling and pleading the athlete to stay interested.

52

The big key to making these work? **Practice.** <u>Over and over and over again</u>. Why? It makes a difference come "game time" when the prospects are real, the objections are tough, and successful negotiations can make the difference between players wanting you to add them to your roster, or you looking in the want ads for a new job.

Part of negotiations sometimes involve waiting, as well. Either you're waiting to decide if you're going to offer them a spot on your team, or they're waiting on making a final decision.

There's almost an art to it, isn't there?

They've taken their visit. You've made your offer.
They've turned in their application. You're crossing your fingers.

And now you wait.

And wait, and wait.

How is there an "art" to it all? Because if you don't successfully play the "waiting game", all your hard work goes down the drain. The time period that many of you find yourself in right now as you read this is **the** critical phase in the recruiting process. The sobering detail of that statement is that most coaches manage the waiting game very, very poorly.

53

Now the good news: I want to give you three, easy-to-implement ideas that work on how to effectively manage this crucial time period in the recruiting process.

Keep giving them the reasons they should compete for you. One big problem we see in athletic departments is the tendency for coaches to stop "selling" their schools, their programs, and themselves. They (not you, but the other coach down the hall) go to their corner, and basically tell their recruits that they'll not bother them anymore until they're ready to make their decision. Some coaches describe this as not wanting to pressure their recruits. On the flip side, your prospects are craving direction. They want good reasons to finally choose you. Make sure you give it to them.

Make sure you are talking to the parents. Why? As most of you know, our **national study** on how prospects make their final decision tells us that parents are one of the key outside influences in a prospect's final decision. So it should make sense that you should be communicating with mom and dad during that awkward silent time that happens during the waiting game. We find that a conversation with the parents can really be insightful, mainly because they will often divulge crucial information about what's going on behind the

54

scenes. Don't forget to include them in good, in-depth communication during this part of the process.

Don't be afraid to set a (reasonable) deadline. By "reasonable" I mean ten days…two weeks…a month… something that doesn't demand an immediate decision. So, what's the point in a longer deadline? Because it's something that gives you some power, coach. Too many of you give it away to the parents, and then complain when they use that power you've given them to make you wait and worry. As we talk about in the workshops we conduct for athletic departments on campuses around the country, someone has to control the sales process (which is what this is). And as the lead sales professional, it's your responsibility to lead that discussion by setting the guidelines for what's allowed and what isn't. A reasonable deadline during this decision making process will give you a yes or a no that will enable you to move forward, and maybe – just maybe – give your prospect a reason to talk to you first and accept your offer.

Should you use these three guidelines? If what you're doing now involves you feeling like you aren't in control of the process, or if your prospect that you have penciled in as your new starting point guard hasn't returned your phone calls in about six weeks, or if you've stopped sending emails and letters selling you and your program they way you did right after you put them on your recruiting list, then I think it might be a smart move.

These strategies work, Coach. All it takes to be successful is a willingness to try something new, and the willingness to take control of these final days of the recruiting process.

56

LESSON EIGHT:

They Didn't Teach You How to Be a Collaborative Negotiator

There are two types of negotiating and recruiting styles that coaches can use when interacting with their prospects. The first, and most common, method is to be a "manipulative negotiator". You see that in the business world quite a bit these days. Manipulative negotiating sees you and your athlete (and their family) as adversaries. Tactics include exerting your power and hiding your own nonverbal communications. There is a lot of mistrust, tension, and suspicion.

When you're a "manipulator" your goal is to win. The focus is on single answers and positions - "This is what I want!" It's hardball negotiating. If you are making a one-time negotiation and you're not going to see the people anymore, perhaps you can get away with it, but it's not a healthy practice when you take into account that you'll be coaching your prospects for years to come.

The *collaborative* negotiator, on the other hand, sees the participants - you and your prospect - as problem solvers looking for a mutually satisfactory solution. It's a process that *both* parties can walk away from and feel comfortable that neither one was "had." It relies on trust, openness, credibility and honesty. The goal is a wise and fair outcome for all parties. The focus is on multiple options, within your reason and budget as a coach. Coaches who take this approach see many ways to satisfy both parties' needs, not just one.

> *Everybody - every coach, every recruiter, every sales professional - should have a well-defined negotiating philosophy.*

You must have a clear vision of what it is you want out of the negotiation (i.e., recruiting phone call, home visit, hosting a campus visit) before you begin that process. Sales and marketing author Tony Alessandra has a negotiating philosophy that he stands by as tried-and-true that works well for college coaches who want to elevate their recruiting approach:

"When two people want to do business with each other, they will not let the details stand in the way. However, when two people do not want to do business with each other, the details will rarely pull the deal together."

58

If a prospect and their family really want to play for you and go to your school, they'll be more apt to give ground and find a way to make compromises if it leads to a chance to play for you. This type of recruiting style is still very much in the minority, which actually should make it even more attractive for anyone reading this book – because it's a rarely used method of negotiating and recruiting among college coaches, those who do use it will really stand-out from their competition.

Are you willing to test the waters and try some collaborative recruiting with a few of your athletes that you're recruiting? If so, here are ten ways for college coaches to become better collaborative recruiters.

Develop a recruiting and negotiation strategy that spells out what you will and won't do during the negotiations. Have a plan. Don't walk into a house without knowing what you're willing to give, and how much. You go into a game with a plan, and you should do the same when it comes to recruiting a prospect.

Collect as much background information as possible beforehand on the prospect, his or her family, his or her

coach and anyone else you'll be facing in the recruiting and negotiation process. The addition of a strong willed individual from one of those groups I just listed changes the dynamics a lot. You need to have a strategy in place to take those potential hurdles and turn them into positives for your position.

Evaluate your competitive exposure. What are the odds that another coach (or coaches) will come up with a better offer than the one you are making? This information can help establish your maximums and minimums when it comes to what you're willing to give the athlete. Don't get caught by surprise when it comes to a competitive offer that may already be in the works or on the table (we covered how best to approach the athlete with this question a few weeks ago...if you need a reminder, just e-mail me).

Prepare and role-play with colleagues _prior_ to your initial recruiting meeting with the prospect and family. It provides you with confidence in facing questions and situations you are now prepared to handle when (not if) they arise. You practice for game-time circumstances all the time...you need to do the same when it comes to getting ready to recruit a prospect.

60

This is one of the most effective ways to perfect your skills, but it is also one of the hardest to follow-through with. You're reading this and thinking, "sounds like a great idea, but I don't want to take the time to practice in front of another coach." Come on, coach! Practice can make all the difference in the world. I know it isn't fun to practice, but getting feedback from a peer can be a huge help in stepping-up your recruiting skills.

5. **Tailor your pace and presentation to the individual differences of the other people.** People who are very relationship oriented and low in assertiveness are called Relaters and are primarily interested in relationships. Those who are "people" oriented and highly assertive are called Socializers and are interested in recognition. Task oriented, highly assertive people are Directors who are concerned about results. Less assertive, task oriented people are Thinkers who like structure. Be flexible in your "approach" with the differences in people. It will reduce relationship tension and subsequently increase interpersonal trust, credibility, cooperation and productivity. When you hear about an athlete that signs with a school because "me and my family just really felt comfortable with the coach" it probably means that the coach recognized the

type of individual they were talking to and adjusted their presentation to fit the other person's style.

Take time to study all dimensions of your prospect's current situation. Ask questions and listen with your ears **and** eyes. Try to determine the end results the other person is attempting to accomplish, not solely his position or demands. However, it is vital to find out the decision-making criteria (must haves vs. should haves vs. nice to haves) of the other person. This will provide you with his/her negotiation limits.

When presenting your offer, try to relate that offer to the end results the other person is attempting to achieve. Show how your program's offer will benefit the prospect. In short, tie everything you can back to the points you discovered in studying all the dimensions of your prospect's current situation to the offer and opportunity that you're presenting to the athlete.

Negotiate the points of difference. Sometimes this is possible, sometimes it isn't. The point here is to find out what the points of difference are, and then talk about ways to "meet in the middle."

62

I wish more coaches would do this...you'd be amazed at the response from athletes when it's done.

9. **Do not "defend" your offer.** Too many coaches are too defensive when it comes to what they're offering, and critical of an athlete who doesn't jump on the first offer. Or, they feel guilty about not being able to offer a full ride scholarship to a particular athlete. Invite criticism and advice. For instance, "What would you do if you were in my position?" That way, the athlete (and more importantly, their parents) feel like you're listening to them and taking their feelings and priorities into account.

At the conclusion of your "negotiations", make sure all parties fully and clearly understand who is to do what, when, where, how, and why. Set up a schedule. Don't leave the meeting with uncertainty. You want a method for how the decision is made, and so does your prospect and his or her family. It's up to you, coach, to set that methodology.

These ten ideas really work well when they're put into practice as a part of an overall recruiting strategy. I've worked personally with coaches who have really perfected becoming "collaborative negotiators" and the one thing they tell me they notice

63

immediately is how appreciative their prospect's family is with the approach.

<u>LESSON NINE</u>:

They Didn't Teach You About "Theoretical Identity Assumption"

Don't worry, we're not going to explore the space-time continuum, or memorize some little known theory of Einstein's. Although, what you learn about this next practical technique could change the way you approach recruiting.

Here's a question for you: Are you finding that the athletes you're recruiting are dragging their feet when it comes to making a decision, or even when it comes to just leveling with you as to where they are in the decision-making process?

You're not alone.

Indecisive prospects are one of the things that make recruiting such a headache for college coaches today. Hunting down and athlete and chasing after a decision is time consuming, and can even be downright discouraging.

So, with that problem in mind, here's a technique you might want to try to get your prospect to come clean with you, or even make that final commitment to your program. It's a sales technique called "Theoretical Identity Assumption". Here's the basics of how it works:

The technique is based on a psychological concept called "Cognitive Dissonance", a psychological term which describes the uncomfortable tension that comes from holding two conflicting thoughts at the same time. More precisely, it is the perception of incompatibility between two cognitions, where "cognition" is defined as any element of knowledge, including attitude, emotion, belief, or behavior.

The theory of "cognitive dissonance" states that contradicting cognitions serve as a driving force that compels the mind to acquire or invent new thoughts or beliefs, or to modify existing beliefs, so as to reduce the amount of dissonance (conflict) between cognitions.

For college coaches who need to sign the best recruits possible, this is the bottom line of it all:

Contradictions in the mind of your athlete are uncomfortable for them.

66

And because they're uncomfortable, they motivate change. If there is a contradiction between a prospect's attitude and actions, he or she is much more likely to change their mind versus their behavior in order to eliminate that discomfort.

A worthwhile recruiting example might be this scenario: You have an athlete who is dragging their feet when it comes to giving you their commitment. A good move on your part, using this technique, might be ask the athlete about a situation you're facing with one of your current players, and you want their advice as someone roughly the same age as your player, on how they would handle it. Tell them that your player isn't sure if they're going to be back at the school next year, and despite your best efforts to get a decision from her she still isn't giving you a final answer - which makes it hard for you to plan for next year.

The logical answer that an athlete should give to that scenario is that it probably isn't fair of the athlete to not let you know what they're doing, and they're putting you in a tough spot because of her indecision. How could that athlete not agree with that line of thinking?

Once they give you the answer to the scenario you're looking for, you might respond by telling them that you're kind of facing the same problem with them as a recruit, and its making for a difficult situation when it comes to planning for next year.

You're simply mirroring your prospect's position...a position that they obviously believe in, as evidenced by the advice that they just gave you in dealing with your current player. That should open the door for a heart-to-heart discussion as to what their intentions are, or what's holding up the decision.

Do you see the example of how cognitive dissonance is working for you here, Coach? You've opened the door for your prospect to state an opinion of what's right and wrong, and then asked them to use the same logical line of thinking when applying it to the situation that you face in recruiting them. You've pointed out a conflict that needs to be resolved, both in their mind as well as in the real world of recruiting priorities that you are responsible for as a college coach.

Is this a better way to get an answer from your prospect? Well, if you had just pushed and pushed and pushed for an answer, and kept pressing for information, your prospect might become defensive and react negatively to the pressure. With the Theoretical Identity Assumption technique, you get your prospect to step back and see the problem from *your* point of view. And, you've done it in a way that is professional and inviting.

Would you use it with every prospect in every situation? No. But there are many instances where this technique can clear a roadblock and open up the lines of communications again with a
68

valued recruit. And, more importantly, it gives you vital information that you need as a coach to map our your recruiting strategy with this prospect and others.

LESSON TEN:

They Didn't Teach You About the Eight Objections Coaches Have to Overcome

It's vital that you overcome objections when you're recruiting.

Why? Because it's the number one reason you lose prospects to the competition: They've done a better job at overcoming a prospect's objections than you have.

The same holds true even if there isn't any competition involved in battling you for the recruit. The coach who doesn't overcome objections in the mind of their prospect, or their prospect's parents, won't be able to sign the athlete even if they are the only program recruiting them.

Objections are a natural part of the sales process, and should be expected by coaches as they go out and recruit student-athletes. Objections are actually a good sign in this respect: They indicate that your interest or offer has them thinking about it, enough at least to come up with some problems with the offer that they want you to help them in overcoming. And make no mistake about it, coach, an objection is a cry for help from your prospect.

70

Here are the eight biggest objections you'll face in recruiting an athlete to your school, and how to attack those objections...and defeat them:

1. Lack of perceived value in your "product". Your school isn't as good as the other one that's recruiting them. Your team didn't do as well in the post-season. The other coach has more championships than you do. All of these things are "product failures" in the eyes of your prospect. Attack this objection by pointing out the positives of your "product" and even agreeing with some of their assessments about your competition. Whatever you do, don't be defensive and tear down the other program that your prospect is offering as a comparison. In the long run, that hurts you.

2. **Lack of perceived urgency in agreeing to what you are offering.** They seldom see the same level of urgency that you do when it comes to committing to your program. They're a laid-back teenager, and you're a coach on a schedule. The trick here is not to pressure them into making a decision...that actually causes *more* hesitation on their part. What you want to do is to be honest and up-front with them: Help them to understand that you have to make decisions on recruits, that you want them to be a part of your program, but that as of a certain date you will have

to move on to someone else. Honesty goes a long way towards winning over a waffling prospect.

3. Perception of inferiority to a competitive program. Similar to the first objection, but a bit different. This objection centers around a direct comparison between you and some other program that you are competing with for the prospect. There are lots of ways to defeat this, but the one that tends to work best for the colleges I consult with is using your "inferiority" as the reason you need the athlete...you need them so that you can raise your program up to the level of the program you are being compared to. You're agreeing with the athlete's assessment of the situation, and then complimenting them by telling them that they are one of the keys for you to become like the higher profile program.

4. The prospect wants something different than the parents. The key for coaches here is to recognize and identify a conflict between the prospect and their parents, and then help to resolve it. This is a touchy one to try and summarize here in a few sentences but you need to make sure you are viewed by both parties as a "problem solver"...someone who will put their sales priorities on the back-burner for a while to help a parent and child come to some kind of agreement on what's best for the athlete, and building yourself as a good choice for that common vision.

72

5. Lack of funds to "purchase" your "product". Different schools at different division levels will handle this uniquely. But make sure, no matter what your scholarship situation is, to identify any financial barriers present in the family as it relates to what you are offering the athlete. There may, in fact, be nothing you can do for them based on those barriers. But, at least you will uncover that objection early on, deal with it the best you can, and then move on to a new prospect if nothing can be accomplished with the original prospect.

6. Personal issue with the decision maker(s). Are there hidden agendas and factors at work against you that you do not yet know? This is a more common factor than most coaches realize...the dream of a father for his son to play at the school he played at, the mom who wants her daughter closer to home, etc. Most of these never get verbalized to you, the coach. If you suspect that something is holding your prospect back from committing, but you just don't know what that could be, simply ask, "Are there any issues that are holding you back that I'm not aware of?" That might just open the door to a very good conversation and lead to a resolution of the problem.

7. **Family's tie to another school or coach.** Similar to the prior point, but different in that this is focused solely on a tie or perceived commitment to another school (like the dad who is

holding out hope for his son to play at the school he played at, even though you know that's not likely to happen based on ability or other factors). The same question used above will do the trick here. But, one word of caution: In dealing with this objection, you may be treading on a father or mother's dream for their child...approach very carefully in how you defeat this objection.

8. "It's safer to do nothing" perception. I've talked to many athletes who are just worn down by the recruiting process, and make the decision to not play college sports or choose the safe route by playing a few years at the local junior college. You need to express empathy for the athlete in this situation, and then ask them this important question: "How will putting-off committing to our program help your athletic career?" That's a tough one to answer...but the answer, whatever it is, should give you some clues as to how to proceed. Or, better yet, it may help them to realize that they need to re-focus on your program as a good avenue for continuing their athletic career.

Is this an exhaustive list? Of course not. However, it's been my experience that these eight types of objections are the most common hurdles a college coach will face when recruiting a prospect. The bottom line: You MUST defeat these objections EVERY TIME when you're recruiting a prospect.

74

LESSON ELEVEN:

They Didn't Teach You Why Rattling Off Your Program's Benefits to Your Prospect Is a Bad Idea

College coaches, like many sales professionals, love to list reasons why their program is "better" than everyone else's. Better stadium, better schedule, better tradition, better weight room, better city, better degrees.

Coaches love bullet-points. The list of benefits. I've seen coach after coach list their program's plusses to me as we work with them to improve their approach. The problem I see? The benefits they're listing are all about them, and not their prospect.

Sales people are the same way. Remember the last time you bought a car? Your salesperson loved to rattle off the many benefits of the that new car that you were looking at. They're usually trained to do so when they begin work for their dealership. The company, you see, is very proud of their benefits and bragging points. And so, like many college coaches, they like to make sure their customers/prospects know about the benefits and falsely believe that those same prospects will be so impressed with the list of benefits that they won't be able to help themselves, and will buy the product or service immediately.

Here's the problem with that line of thinking...

Your prospects actually don't care all that much about your list of benefits, accomplishments and accolades. I know that might hurt your feelings, but its the surprising truth.

Why do coaches feel compelled to list off as many benefits as possible to the kids they are recruiting?

1. **Coaches thinks it makes sense**. Our gut tells you that the more bragging rights you can list off compared to your competition puts you in the better position to win the recruit. Seems logical...the coach that can list the most benefits wins, right?

2. **It's a lot easier.** Once you come up with all the positives of your program, its easy to memorize that list and recite the positives to your prospects. What's harder? To connect the prospect's needs with what your program can offer (more on that in a moment).

3. **Coaches like to brag.** You're an athlete at heart. You want to compete and win in the war for recruits, and bragging rights

76

tend to get worn on the sleeves of proud coaches - sometimes to their detriment.

The big problem with rattling off benefits? Your prospects, as I said earlier, don't care all that much about them. I didn't say they don't care at all, I said they just didn't care that much. What are they more concerned with? How your program gives *them* what *they* are looking for. How your program helps *them* achieve *their* dreams. When you give them your non-stop list of benefits and bragging rights, you force your prospect connect their own dots as to how those benefits relate or matter to them. Maybe they will, maybe they won't.

The big question that your prospects are asking themselves is, "Why should I care?" They're also wondering, "What's in all this for *me*?

That's a good question for you to ask yourself, coach. Take a look at the list of things you usually tell your prospects about when it comes to your program. Now, after you list each thing, ask yourself, "Why should my prospect care?" If you can't come up with a good reason a teenage kid would care about what you just told them, maybe you shouldn't stress it so much.

My recommendation? Include the answer to their "Why should I care?" question along with the benefit or bragging point your telling them about. For example, "We've had eight players turn pro over the last ten years. That means that all of our players -

77

including you - will get the best coaching your sport has to offer, and we'll do everything we can to give you the chance to play at the next level." **You listed the benefit, and then told them <u>why</u> they should care about that benefit.**

So, all of this begs the question: How can you get a recruit to actually anticipate your selling points? Simple. Just remember back to when you were a little kid, Coach.

The night of Christmas Eve, lots of little kids are full of anticipation.

The thought of toys under the tree, some extra sugar in their bellies, and just the overall fun and excitement of what the holidays brings is almost too much for them to handle. If you doubt me, I'll let you talk to the 7-year old boy in our house who has spent the last week trying (and failing) to guess what's under the wrapping paper in those boxes under the tree with his name on them.

What many coaches miss in that scene being repeated in homes around the country is the incredible power of that anticipation, and how it changes the emotions, thinking and general outlook kids who can't wait for Christmas morning. More specifically, many coaches miss the lesson that they can take away and apply to their recruiting efforts.

78

The reason we talk about the importance of creating a "feeling" in the story that you tell your recruits is because they rely on those powerful emotions to make their final decision much of the time. You and I can agree that this isn't always the smartest way to choose a college or program, but there's little doubt that it occurs on a regular basis in the recruiting process – at least according to our research.

So as a serious recruiter looking to connect with a prospect you really want, shouldn't you want to create the same energy and excitement around your contact with a recruit, as well as how they view your program emotionally while making their final decision? If so, building anticipation – and understanding the components of why it's such a powerful force – should be something that you aim to do in your recruiting message.

Here's how you do it:

Your prospect will anticipate your next message more if you lead into it with the previous message. One of the key principles we put to work in creating effective recruiting campaigns for our clients is the idea that messaging should be ongoing, and sequential. In other words, one message should set up the next message…and so on, and so on, and so on. Too many messages we see from coaches are all encompassing, one-size-fits-all behemoths that tend to overwhelm and bore their teenage recipient. Coaches need to start focusing on

79

breaking up their longer messages into shorter, easier to digest stories that build into the next message rather than answer every single question right away. That's one of the big keys to anticipation in recruiting.

Your prospect will anticipate talking to you if you exceed their expectations. Too often, a coach will jeopardize an interaction with a recruit by falling-back on the same tired, boring, run-of-the-mill conversation points that recruited athletes tell us they dread: "What movies are you watching", "What did you download on iTunes this week", "did anything great happen at school this week"…you get the picture, Coach. When you earn the privilege of having a one-on-one talk with your recruit, you'd better try to figure out a way to amaze them if you want to keep positive anticipation on your side with them. Are you asking questions no one else is? Are you going to reveal an important "next step" you want them to take in the process? Will you go over their strengths and weaknesses from the last time you watched them play? Can you update them on any part of the process on your campus regarding their application? ALL of that builds importance and value in their conversation with you…this time *and* the next time. (By the way, you'll know you have let *negative* anticipation seep into the relationship when your calls go to voicemail, or they aren't returning your emails as much as they used to).

80

Your prospect will anticipate coming to campus if they have been given exciting peeks at what awaits them when they get there. Have you teased your recruit and given them glimpses of what your team is like, what campus is like, why he or she would want to see the dorms, and what the area is like around your college? Those are some of the key elements our research has uncovered as to what triggers that "anticipation" in the minds of your recruits when it comes to the risky, scary idea of committing to a campus visit. Recruits will rarely visit a campus without a good reason that is solidified in their mind – either one that they came up with on their own, or a picture that you have painted for them over a period of time.

One more thing:

Since we're building-out these concepts using the excitement of presents under the tree during Christmas and the holidays, think about what happens *after* they open the presents. There's an almost immediate "crash". The anticipation and excitement is gone, and all that's left is a pile of toys, the hand-knit underwear their Aunt Edna sent them, and wrapping paper strewn all over the place. The energy is gone – as is that valuable anticipation.

If you're a parent, watch what happens Christmas morning after the presents are all opened. You'll see what I'm talking about.

The point I'm making is that you need to anticipate that, Coach. That means after they visit campus, for example, *you* need to anticipate that they will need a clear picture of what the next step in your process is in order to maintain their focus and excitement about the idea of competing for you. My personal observation is that coaches tend to take an optimistic view of their recruit, picturing that with each step they take in the recruiting process he or she becomes more and more excited, and naturally wants to talk more about competing for you. In the majority of cases, I find that the opposite is true: The anticipated is now the familiar, and they'll search out a new source of anticipation and excitement in the form of another program (remember that recruit who got spotted late by a competitor and rushed through the process to commit with them?...That's a prime example of a kid continuing to look for anticipation and excitement in the form of another program).

Your job, Coach, is to put a focus on managing the experience and continuing to build that anticipation in your recruits' mind. If you can master that art, while being careful not to just rattle off your selling points to prospects, you'll solve a key riddle when it comes to how to ride that wave of anticipation in the recruiting process.

LESSON TWELVE:

They Didn't Teach You About "SPIN Selling", and Why It's So Effective

What is "SPIN Selling"? Only one of the most effective sales techniques developed over the past decade or so.

It's an extremely popular sales strategies developed for corporate sales teams, and is taught in most Fortune 500 sales training programs. Why? *It works.*

"SPIN" is an acronym for **Situation, Problem, Implication** and **Need-Payoff.** Incorporating those four aspects into your daily recruiting efforts can pay off the same big dividends enjoyed by some of the nation's most successful sales professionals.

Here's how to do it:

Whenever you're talking to a prospective athlete, incorporate the components of SPIN Selling into your conversations. Just follow the acronym step-by-step:

Situation - Ask a question related to your prospect's situation. Good example questions might include, "How many other schools are recruiting you? How much money do you have saved for college? What is your biggest goal when it comes to playing sports in college? What's your vision for your athletic career in college?" These types of questions are usually easy for a college coach to come up with during a recruiting conversation. You may have some good questions that you always ask. The key is not stopping with a situation-based questions, but building on your prospect's answer to this first stage question.

Problem - These questions are designed to uncover the pain experienced by your prospect regarding the situation question you just asked. To be a successful recruiter, you need to successfully link the problem or "pain" that your prospect is experiencing with the solution that you're offering in the form of a scholarship or opportunity to play at your school. Let's assume that your prospect's answer to our first situation question ("How many other schools are recruiting you?") is, "There's only one other school I've heard from other than you, coach." Your response to that might be, "What concerns you about the lack of interest from other schools?" Or, "What would your plan be if no other schools showed interest in you?" Again, you're trying to underscore a problem in the mind of your prospect. Getting them to

84

verbalize that problem is an important step in the process of connecting with your prospect.

Implication - As the title suggests, this question will imply a result of the problem and situation that your prospect face. Some college coaches I've worked with this past year have had a tendency to try and combine their "problem" and "implication" questions, or skip one in the process. Don't do it! Make sure you ask each question separately. Sticking with our example, a good implication question would be, "Would you be able to go to college if you didn't get some athletic scholarship money from a college?" or, "What would you feel like if you couldn't play your sport again after you graduate from high school?" Emphasizing the implications of a potential problem begins to help your prospect connect the dots in their mind, and will put you in a position of strength as you head into the final part of the SPIN Selling equation.

Need-Pay Off - The key here is to make your solution (your offer, your program, you as a coach, your college, etc.) the logical choice of your prospect to solve the problem that they've just verbalized to you. A good example Need-Pay Off question or statement might be, "Would you feel relieved if we were able to put together a package for you that would ensure you could play college sports after high school?" Or, you could simply ask "How could I show you that our program would be the best solution for that problem?" One more: "What would you need to hear from me to cause you to commit to our program so that you wouldn't have to worry about money for college?"

Finished with one particular question? Go back and ask another probing, open-ended question by starting the SPIN Selling process from the start. You can use SPIN Selling with every prospect you're recruiting, and with every situation that applies to their life.

Does it take practice? Absolutely. Is it worth it? You bet it is. If you become comfortable asking those types of questions, you'll find that you'll be in control of the recruiting process from the start and form a deeper relationship with every prospect you talk to.

LESSON THIRTEEN:

They Didn't Teach You How to Make Time for Recruiting Your Prospects

In talking with coaching staffs and athletic directors from around the country, on campuses both big and small, without exception one of the biggest hurdles that coaches seem to be facing is finding enough time to do everything they need to do when it comes to recruiting.

"I'm up against it for time, Dan", said one assistant coach I met with during a break at one of our workshops. "I'm here until 9 o'clock most weekday evenings, and I still can't seem to get everything done!" His comments seemed to be shared by his fellow coaches, both at his school and other schools that I've had the opportunity to visit.

After one of our training sessions at a Division II campus was completed not too long ago, I used an empty athletic department office to check my e-mail and return a few phone calls. What I observed over the next hour or so was amazing…

Two coaches spent about twenty minutes talking about their upcoming vacations in a little lounge area. I overheard another coach on the phone talking to an old friend she used to coach with. Later on that afternoon, after I had met with their athletic director for an early dinner, I noticed three coaches casually talking in an office.

Now I know that there are lots of necessary conversations that take place in a normal work day. But I also know - from my own experience as an experienced workplace time-waster - that a lot of valuable time gets eaten away by trivial, unimportant interruptions and distractions. So it stands to reason that if you are able to do away with a few bad habits, you'd probably be able to have more time to get the important job of recruiting done (with time to spare!).

Here are six ways you can make more time for recruiting, without adding more hours to your already hectic workday:

Make a list the night before. Start your recruiting day the night before by making a list of the top five or ten things you plan to accomplish in your recruiting duties for the upcoming day. Writing down the things you know you need to do will let you sleep more

88

soundly, and give you a clear direction the next morning when your day starts. Try it. I think this is one of the simple foundations for being much more productive during your day.

Do as much of your recruiting-related tasks first thing in the morning. Whether its e-mails to send, letters to write, updating social media sites or making arrangements for an upcoming prospect campus visit, get it done right when you walk into the office. Plenty of fires flare-up as the day progresses, and it seems like the first thing to get shoved aside is recruiting. Get your recruiting tasks done first thing in the morning, working from the list you made the night before.

Turn off your e-mail. Check it first thing in the morning, once in the afternoon, and then again at the end of the day whenever possible. Leaving your e-mail open and on your computer screen throughout the day is one of the biggest time wasters known to coaches. You think you're being productive snapping quick replies back to your senders, but in reality you are distracting yourself from a multitude of other important recruiting tasks (and other coaching responsibilities) that are much more important.

Make recruiting "measurable". Set small daily goals for yourself when it comes to recruiting, and then check to see if you met those goals. Maybe you set the goal of calling at least one new high school coach to expand your network of eyes and ears out looking for talent for your program. Or, maybe its to hand write five prospects by the end of the day. Whatever it is, set your goals and then post them in front of you so that you make sure you accomplish them. Measure your success in recruiting effectiveness in the same way you would analyze your team's statistics as a way of measuring their performance.

Schedule the rest of your day in 15-minute intervals. The only way to use the time you're saving from the first four steps is to stick to a schedule the rest of the day. Measure out your day in blocks of time, and schedule yourself for whatever it is you need to do down to the quarter hour. Very few coaches do this on a regular basis when I first meet them, but those that do learn these methods are much happier and a lot more productive when it comes to their jobs as college coaches.

Establish it as a top priority. One big reason you don't seem to have enough time for recruiting is that you still haven't embraced it as one of the most important parts of your career as a college coach. In fact, when you're not in-season, I think I could argue that it is THE most important part of your coaching career. Most coaches haven't established recruiting, and all the little details that are a part of it, as a top priority in their day. They let interruptions, distractions, unimportant conversations and unwanted visitors eat up their time. Don't let that happen to you. These bad habits have killed lots of up-

90

and-coming business careers, and they can kill your promising coaching career as well.

Mandy Green, a Division I head soccer coach and regular contributor to our conferences and College Recruiting Weekly newsletter on the topic of time management, offered this tip on what works for her and many of the other college coaches when it comes to important recruiting tasks:

> *"I schedule a set hour or hour and a half almost every day to do nothing but recruiting emails. I shut my door so I don't get interrupted. I turn off my auto indicator on my email screen so I am not distracted by new emails coming in. I don't stop to do other tasks that I remember to do (I write them down on a master to to-do list so I get it out of my head but don't forget to do it), and I turn down the volume on my phone so I don't hear when a new text message or phone call may come in. Recruiting emails, that's it.*
>
> *I try to eliminate as many distractions as I can so I can concentrate all my attention on exactly one thing and one thing only. To reach the state of flow at work you need to be totally focused at your task and not distracted every three minutes.*

Getting to the point where I am even doing all of this has taken me a few years' worth of trial and error. The set-up doesn't take me long anymore because I have been gotten into the habit now. Each step individually helped save some time here and there. When I do all of these things at once, it is like recruiting email nirvana. I love it. I spend a lot less time on my email but I can get so many more emails out. I am more in control of the recruiting process. I am not as overwhelmed anymore. Of course, I still have bad days with it. But adding more structure to the set-up process of doing recruiting emails has saved a lot of time for me."

Easy to do? Surprisingly, no. Most coaches will look at the list, and the example given by Coach Green, and kind of roll their eyes because its all just common sense, much of which they have heard before. Yet, those same coaches will let their valuable work day slip away because they haven't made it a priority to keep focused on what it is that they need to do to be successful recruiters.

Are you struggling to find time to get your recruiting done in a more efficient manner? Does the thought of not stressing-out to sign more quality recruits sound appealing? Want more time away from the coaching office to spend with your spouse and kids?

It's all there waiting for you, coach. But first, you need to get serious about <u>using the time you already have</u> to do your recruiting.

<u>LESSON FOURTEEN</u>:

They Didn't Teach You About the Ripple Effect of Treating Your Prospect Poorly

This is a true story.

I happened to have a conversation at an airport with a parent. I was coming back home after conducting an On-Campus Workshop on the East coast, and struck up a conversation with a dad who was traveling back home with his son after attending a football camp at a highly respected Division I school.

Dad wasn't happy. They had traveled 1500 miles to the camp at the invitation of an assistant coach who was recruiting him. When the athlete got to the school, he felt "unwanted". The assistant coach, who was chummy with the athlete during a brief visit to the athlete's school a month earlier, hardly said a word. The head coach never said hello or introduced himself. No tour of the school. Nothing "special" that would set that school apart

94

from the other ten Division I schools that seem to be seriously recruiting the athlete.

Now, it's one thing to change your mind about an athlete you're recruiting and cool-off your pursuit of him or her. But unbeknownst to the coaching staff at the school, their poor treatment of the athlete and his father resulted in this:

· The dad and athlete talked about the experience in a negative way with two other recruits and their dads who were in for camp. They had similar experiences, and all agreed it effected the way they looked at the program.

· The athlete has crossed the team of his list of colleges he was considering.

· The dad, who has a blog, is talking about the trip and the program in a less than favorable way. That means other recruits and their parents might read it.

· The athlete has already told another incoming junior at his school, who was getting the same look from this same D1 football program, that they were "jerks" and that he "should forget about going there."

My point in relating this story to you?

Simple: No matter what your sport, camps and other in-person campus interactions are a recruiting mainstay at most colleges around the country. And even if by chance you don't run a camp as a part of your program, you're probably bringing your prospects on campus.

Here are a few things you need to be doing with <u>each and every athlete</u> you come in contact with:

Thank them for coming, and tell them you're glad they're here. If the well known head coach at this D1 football program would have taken the 4.5 seconds to do that with the athlete I talked about above, they'd still be on his list. Instead, the prospect felt ignored. And that was all it took to give him a reason to cross that school off his list.

Recognize out of area athletes. They've traveled far and made an effort to come to your camp. They deserve to get a special "thank you" from your staff.

Be honest with your prospect. If they've dropped off your radar, let them know. Be honest and up-front with them. In talking with this dad and his son, they would have had no problem with hearing that news. What they did have a problem with was feeling like they were unwanted after being invited to the camp personally by the coach. Be honest with them, coach. They can take it, and you'll maintain your respect with the prospect.

96

Wake up! It's not 1970! In the "good old days" a coach had all the control (and we all got to enjoy those groovy 1970's fashions!), What happened at a camp or campus visit stayed there. Today, it's a different world. Recruiting media and websites keep track of every up and down of campus visits and prospect leanings - if the athletes themselves don't Tweet each up and down. You're under a microscope, coach. Doesn't matter if you're a high profile D1 or a small D3. Athletes (and especially savvy parents) talk. And with the advent of blogs and the Internet, your private recruiting blunders become public conversation.

Take a good hard look at how you treat your recruits on campus. *ALL of them.* Each one needs to be viewed as a mouthpiece for your program. Expect them to take their experience at your school back to their town, where they'll talk about you (positively or negatively) with their teammates and coaches.

Not making your prospect's parents feel special? You'd better. Teenagers might shy away from being too critical publicly of a particular program, but parents usually aren't. Likewise, if they were treated well, both will go back home and talk about their positive experience.

As the title of this lesson says, it's a "ripple effect". Is that a good or bad thing for you and your program?

<u>LESSON FIFTEEN</u>:

They Didn't Teach You That Every Now and Then, You Just Need to Refocus On the Fundamentals

When you've been in college coaching for a while, you tend to get tunnel vision when it comes to your approach, your program and how to get recruits to visit campus. It's hard to see through the day to day, month to month, year to year grind that a college coaching career can become. Because of that, your recruiting skills can start to stagnate.

So every so often, you probably need to sit down and refocus on some recruiting fundamentals. As a coach, its something you do with your athletes from time to time. A good salesperson also does once in a while. They will work with a mentor, read a good book on selling, attend a sales seminar...things that re-connect them with the basics.

So here are a few check-up questions for you, coach:

98

- *How's your recruiting going?*
- *How's the roster for next year's recruiting class looking?*
- *Are you connecting with your prospects?*

Are you signing the kids you *really* want, or is it another year of settling for athletes that you had to bring in just to field a team?

Let's go back to some fundamentals. Let's make sure you're doing everything that a good sales professional - and a good recruiter - will do day in, day out, with every single prospect. See if there's anything you're missing in your approach when you're recruiting athletes for your program:

Asking good questions. It's one of the most talked-about aspects of recruiting here at Selling for Coaches. With our members, and during our seminars, effective questioning ranks at the top of subjects coaches really want to master. Are you asking good probing questions? Good "trial close" questions? If you aren't asking really effective questions, you're probably struggling at recruiting really good athletes.

Being an active listener. When you listen to a prospect's answer to your really good question, are you hearing them? In other words, are you understanding what they're saying "between the

99

lines"? Are you using their information in asking effective, probing follow-up questions? Are you linking their answers to the positives that your program offers? Active listening goes hand-in-hand with asking good questions.

Qualifying the mutual benefits. Are you striving to point out the mutual "win wins" for you and the athlete if they were to choose your program? It's always a good idea to verbally state those observations when they become apparent to you (because they may not be apparent to your prospect!)

Discovering your prospect's hot buttons. Are you actively looking for what the athlete is really looking for in a college offer? In a college program? In a coach? How about the parents...are you finding out what matters to them as they decide whether you're the coach that will be the surrogate parent to their child for the next four years? If you're a good recruiter, you should be able to list two or three "hot buttons" for each prospect you're actively recruiting.

Building rapport with your prospect. Have you made a connection? Can you and your prospect, as well as you and your prospect's parents, spend time talking about something other than sports, a scholarship, or your college? Have you taken the time to get to know them in a personal way?

100

Establishing a level of trust. Hard to do if you haven't built rapport first. Have you demonstrated to your prospect that they can trust you? How? Do the parents trust what you're saying? Would you trust you if you were listening to you? Without trust and rapport, you won't sign one single talented recruit.

Establishing credibility. What have you said or done to establish yourself as a coach who they would want to play for? Why should they hand over their athletic development and sports career to you? What's so great about you as a coach that would get them excited about playing for you and becoming a better athlete under your direction?

Developing a valuable relationship. What's "in it" for the prospect, and his or her family, to align themselves with you and your program? Have you clearly established the benefits (scholarship money, playing time, prestige of the school) for the prospect? They need to see the value in you, your program, and your offer.

Handling objections. I've said before that leaving an unanswered objection on the table will probably result in the loss

101

of that prospect. At the very least, leaving an objection unanswered in the mind of your prospect will make it all the more difficult to get that athlete to make the final commitment to your program. Do you handle every objection? Do you re-direct those questions into benefit statements? Are there unanswered questions hanging over the heads of your prospects? Get them answered...quick...or wave goodbye to your prospects.

Mutually planning the next steps. Professors hand out a syllabus at the beginning of a class to give an outline to their students. Do you do the same for your prospects? Do they understand how you'll be making your decision on whether or not to make an offer? Do you understand how they'll be making their decision on whether or not to accept your offer? Come up with a plan, mutually agree on it, and then move forward.

Confirm understanding of the plan. Once you come up with the plan, make sure they understand it. Make sure you understand how their decision is going to be made. Ask over and over again. Make sure you understand all the factors going into their decision.

102

Ask for referrals. Most coaches don't do this. They don't ask about other overlooked players on the prospect's team. Or star players on the lower levels. Or standout athletes that play other sports (what would another coach in your department do if you brought back information on a star player that they didn't know about?...that's got to be worth a lunch or something!) Don't stop recruiting. Ever. Always look for more opportunities.

Look for ways to be their problem solvers. Ultimately, your prospect is looking for an answer to their problems: Financial, athletic...they have problems that they want you to help them solve. Are you helping them with their financial aid forms? Recommending a good off-season training program? If you solve their problems, they'll be loyal to you. Every single time.

Assessing your strengths and weaknesses. With each recruit, can you name the strong points to your offer? Can you list the weak points that are going to be hurdles for you in recruiting the athlete? Once you assess the strengths and weaknesses of your position, work to accentuate the strengths and chip away at the weaknesses. To do that, you have to be a problem solver and answer all of their objections.

103

Affirming a commitment. When you get a commitment, do you tell your prospect that they've made a good decision? Do you still recruit them and sell the positives to them? Or, do you breath a sigh of relief, say "just sign here" and move on to the next prospect? Reaffirm their decision, coach. Make them feel good about it. Make them know that they made the right decision, and never ever let "buyers remorse" settle in.

Expect positive results. Last but not least, coach, be positive. Have a positive attitude when it comes to your recruiting, your program, your abilities, your school and your department. Your attitude shows (more than you think it does) and can effect you - for better or worse - in your recruiting, and your coaching.

Sixteen vital components to each and every prospect you're handling. If you find yourself struggling at being the best recruiter you can be, refer back to this list and check to see if you're off the mark in any of these categories.

104

LESSON SIXTEEN:

They Didn't Teach You How to Successfully Build Trust with Your Top Recruit

Most of us don't like interacting with people we don't feel like we can trust.

The reason we don't trust the telemarketer that calls us is because we don't know her, and it doesn't feel right that a complete stranger should be calling us at home to sell us something.

The reason we don't click on 999 out of 1,000 pop-up advertisements on the Internet is because we remember the time we were burned before when we accidentally downloaded a virus on our computer.

The reason we don't like to go shopping for new cars is because we know we're going to feel pressured by a salesman who gives us the feeling that he's being less than truthful about the promises he's making to us.

And that gut reaction we all have to each of those three scenarios has big implications for college coaches.

If this is the time of year you might find yourself reassessing how you interact with your recruits, and figuring out how effective it is (or isn't), it's important to understand that the same factors you use to judge the trustworthiness of telemarketers, pop-up ads, or car salesmen, are being used by your teenage prospects – and their parents – to judge your trustworthiness. And, like you, they're figuring out whether or not to have a serious interaction with you based on whether they feel like they can trust you or not.

This is important to understand, Coach: The decision to interact happens *before* your recruit actually listens to what you have to say. How you construct your letters, what you say in your emails, and how you interact with them on social media will determine whether or not you get to communicate with that recruit.

And you might be surprised at how many different types of interactions factor into whether or not your recruit chooses to trust you enough to communicate with you. Here are a few of the most important:

106

Your direct interaction between you and your recruit: Did the recruit see how you coached at a camp they attended? How did you act when they watched practice during that unofficial visit? The way your recruit feels about that momentary experience will alter their interaction with you, either positively or negatively. If you're reaching out and communicating with them for the first time, you can bet that the way your message is worded is going to determine whether or not they feel you're worth the interaction.

What they've heard about you: If your recruit heard good things about you from people he or she knows, the entire relationship changes. You automatically get the benefit of the doubt. So, it begs the question: What are you doing to make sure that your current team, former recruits, and the parents of all of those student-athletes, are saying good things about you to your future prospects? (It's an important question, because we find that they are almost always talking about you. The only thing you can control is what they're saying).

What your website, social media and email templates look like: When they look at those properties, what is the brand image that comes to their mind? If you're a smaller school, do you look like the bigger brand programs? If you're one of the bigger programs, how

107

are you separating yourself from your other big-name competitors? Serious question, Coach.

Your tone of voice: This has everything to do how your message (your letter, your email, your phone call) sounds. When you're writing your message, does it sound like you would if you were talking face to face with your prospect? Or, does it sound so formal that your recruit is going to know it's the typical, mass mail, non-personal message that they're used to? Also, are you patient and not rushing your recruit? Are you pushing too early? Urgency rarely leads to increased trust from your recruit. Make sure you are messaging your recruit **the right way**.

Whether you sound scarce, or plentiful: Ever wonder why we recommend a fair but firm deadline in most circumstances? Because it works. If you're the coach that gives a recruit all the time in the world, and lets them know that they can make the decision any time they want, expect to come across as a program that will take anyone at anytime. For most coaches, that doesn't work. You need to find some kind of "scarcity" to talk about with your recruits. Scarcity leads to action.

The size of the commitment you're asking for: If you're asking me to reply to your email early in the recruiting process, there's a good chance that's going to happen. On the contrary, coaches who want

108

long conversations on the phone right away struggle to get a recruit to respond. Coaches who jump into an early conversation about a campus visit might be going too fast, too soon. Be mindful of what you're asking them to do, and how early in the recruiting process you're asking for it.

Your offer: What's in it for your recruit to listen to what you're asking them to commit to? It's a simple but serious question.

Their fear: As we talk about extensively in our workshops for coaches, your recruit's fear is present throughout the recruiting experience. What are you doing to answer that fear? How are you doing that early on, as well as late in the process?

What they see about you online: What they read when they Google you, and how well you post on Twitter, Facebook and Instagram, matter. It matters a lot, Coach. Your online presence is one of the most immediate impressions that gets formed by your recruit. And in most cases, it helps to determine how much interaction they wish to have with you.

How aligned with them you are: How are you proving that you are just like they are, and understand where they're coming from? More importantly, how are you communicating that?

Your honesty: This generation of recruits and their parents are actively searching for coaches who prove they are honest. It's vital that you demonstrate that honesty, and showcase it to them through your messaging. You need to repeatedly demonstrate that you are the coach they can trust. The coaches who are trusted get the best athletes at the end of the day.

How consistent you are in your recruiting efforts: How long have you been showing up? That's an important question in the mind of your prospect. When we **work with clients**, and take their team through a series of focus group questions to determine how best to help formulate their recruiting strategy, one of the most common themes that stands out as being vitally important to recruits is how consistent a coach is in the way they communicate. If you are the coach who sends a couple of messages at the start, and then is hit-and-miss during the rest of the recruiting process, you're probably going to get labeled as inconsistent. And as our research shows, that's going to hurt you as your prospect reaches their final decision.

Since you're going to be judged by this generation of recruits, doesn't it make sense to make sure you're taking an intelligent, thorough approach when it comes to sending out a message that prompts interaction?

That's how trust with your recruit is built. Start now, Coach.

110

LESSON SEVENTEEN:

They Didn't Teach You About "Stitching" and "Story Time" in Your Recruiting Messages

The secret to great recruiting letter and email writing?

"Stitching" and "Story Time".

Let me explain...

These two tricks-of-the-trade are simple and super-effective. Why? <u>Because they ensure that your writing flows nicely, and that it's easily understood by the reader</u>. Doesn't that sound like two good goals to have for any message you are creating for a prospect you want for your program?

We use them all the time as we do work for our clients who are a part of our Total Recruiting Solution client program, and they are part of the principles we teach during our On-Campus Workshops we give to college coaches around the country. And, we've seen the results: More responses and more real interest from recruits.

Here's what they are, and why they work...

111

"Stitching". That's the not-so-technical term for adding a short phrase in between major themes and paragraphs that help tie on idea to the next. Think of it as a verbal knot that "stitches" sections of your letter or email together, and keeps the reader moving to the next thought.

Want an example? I used two very simple forms of the principle in this chapter: Near the top of this story, I wrote "Let me explain..." I devoted a single line to it, so that you - my reader - would see it, recognize that I was about to give you some more information that you would be interested in, and lead you to the next section of text. Then, just before this section on "Stitching", I teased you with a double-promise when I told you that you would find out "what they are, and why they work."

The principle is simple: You want your high school prospect to keep on reading your letter or email, so every once in a while you'll need to re-focus their attention on what you are talking about and the points you are trying to make. A proven way to do it is by "stitching" your ideas together with short phrase like the one's I just used. Here are some others we recommend:

"And that's just the beginning..."

"But better yet..."

"Here's the deal..."

112

"It all boils down to this..."

"Listen, there's more..."

As you begin this year's next recruiting campaign, consider editing your current letters and emails and insert some of these stitching techniques to ensure that your reader stays with you all the way through your message.

"Story Time".

This is one of the best things a coach can do with their message, and yet as I type these words I know that fewer than 2% of coaches that are reading this book will take the steps to make it happen. So, for those of you that do, you'll have a message that sounds better and is more effective than the other 98%.

What you need to do, *after* you apply the "stitching" technique to your text, is to give it to someone else - a fellow coach, your spouse...whoever - and have them read your message back to you. Don't coach them on how it is supposed to sound, just let them read it as they understand it.

What's the point? You will hear how your prospect is going to take in the message, and how it's going to sound to them in their mind as they read it. If you don't like how it sounds as you have it read back to you, then you should re-edit the text immediately and start the process over again. You will eventually end up with

113

text that flows beautifully, and a message that sinks in more deeply and with greater long term impact.

Two simple techniques that are <u>proven</u> to work...and can fit into any budget, last I checked!

Take a good, long look at how your recruiting messages sound in their current form. Then, use these two techniques to make them easier to read and more likely to work. As you begin another year of recruiting a new class of prospects, seeing those two results will make an impact on the rate at which you sign those "next level athletes" that you so desperately want..and need.

114

<u>LESSON EIGHTEEN</u>:

They Didn't Teach You How to Ask the Right Kinds of Questions

It's the core of every good recruiting effort...the single thing that can determine whether you get the prospect, or lose them to a competitor.

Questions.

Especially asking the right ones, the right way, at the right time. That's why I wanted to end the book with this important topic. And, even though we've touched on it throughout the book, there are plenty of reasons why every coach needs to master this aspect of the recruiting process.

Why? Because when you get right down to it, questions drive successful recruiting efforts. Everything else - all those exciting brochures (not), all those sizzling one page letters - don't measure up to really effective questions.

115

To make sure this ends up as a successful year of recruiting for you and your program, I wanted to give you a few of the right kinds of questions you should be asking your prospects right away. See if you can incorporate these into your recruiting conversations as you head into the recruiting season's stretch run:

1. The Who Question

Never, _ever_ assume that the prospect you are speaking with is the real decision-maker.

It sounds strange, but it is true: Your prospect may be only one of a number of individuals who will figure into his or her final decision. Parents, coaches and others may have real influence over your prospect.

Know all the players in the game so you can prepare strategies and tactics to deal with them and how they may individually effect your prospect's decision. Your challenge is to find out if there are other participants in the decision without putting your recruit on the spot. If you're too blunt, the prospect might mislead you. Here is a simple question that you can't live without. Use it every time:

"Amanda, apart from yourself, who is involved in your decision?"

116

Here's a variation: "Kevin, when a player like you has to make a big decision like this, there are usually several people involved. Apart from yourself, who else will help you make your decision?"

You absolutely need to be sure you answer the "who" question first and foremost. No other answer you get during the recruiting process will be more important to uncover.

2. The When Question

I am amazed at how many coaches and recruiters ignore this powerful and insightful question:

"Kathy, when do you see the final decision being made?" Or, "Chad, if our offer was a go in your mind, when do you see it happening?"

The "when" question helps you to assess your prospect's urgency. A decision that will be made within a week has more urgency than a decision that will be made in three months. Knowing when the recruiting might conclude helps you set priorities, determines the time and effort you devote and dictates your follow up strategy with the prospect you're recruiting.

3. The Scenario Question

Discovering a prospect's needs can be challenging in the early stages of recruiting. When prospects don't know you, they tend to be much more reserved in the information they share. Many are not comfortable telling you about their "warts and blemishes" (i.e., their needs, challenges, weaknesses and concerns) until you've established some rapport. You've probably noticed that by now, right coach?

To get around this hesitancy, coaches should use a scenario question. As the name implies, the scenario question paints a scenario that addresses a problem or concern without putting the prospect on the spot. Here are a couple of examples:

"Eric, a lot of the prospects we're recruiting this year have said they're interested in committing as early as possible. Let me ask you, is that something you're thinking about also?"

"Jennifer, we are getting more and more feedback from our prospects that are part of our upcoming recruiting class about who they'll rely on to help them make their final decision. Let me ask you, how would you answer that question?"

The scenario question is based on the premise that "misery loves company". You want the prospect to think, "Gee, if others are experiencing the same thing then it's okay for me to open up."

118

Master the scenario question and you'll get to their needs and inner motivations more quickly, reduce your recruiting cycle and get more recruits committed in less time.

4. The Net Impact Question

Even if you use a scenario question and the recruit opens up to you, it doesn't necessarily mean that the their need for what you're offering at your college is strong enough for him to take positive action. One of the best questions you can ask to determine the depth and breadth of a need your athletic prospect has is the "net impact" question. Here are two versions:

"So what's the net impact of our offer to cover half of your total tuition costs?" Or, "What's the possible net impact of waiting until late March to give us your final decision?"

The net impact forces your prospect to think about the rippling effect of a problem. It gets your prospect to do some analysis. In effect, you want him to say, "Gee, I never thought of it like that." Suddenly, seemingly minor problems become more significant. Or, you learn the net impact is minor in the mind of your teenage prospect. If so, avoid wasting your time. Move on. Because the question is opened-end it gets your client to expand and elaborate. You get information and information is power.

Those four questions alone should generate a lot of insights into the mind of your prospect. How you use that insight is up to you, but savvy coaches will alter their recruiting strategy based on the types of answers they get to these types of questions.

About Tudor Collegiate Strategies

Dan Tudor and his team at Tudor Collegiate Strategies trains college coaches how to recruit more effectively. We do that through training our clients to master cutting edge sales, marketing and communication skills – the same skills that Fortune 500 companies teach their sales professionals to use on a daily basis.

If you're a coach who wants the edge in recruiting, Tudor Collegiate Strategies can help. Visit www.dantudor.com for information and training resources that you can use to become a dominant recruiter.

If you are a coach who really wants that extra edge, consider becoming a Premium Member or Total Recruiting Solution client. You'll receive expanded training, special offers, and exclusive access to the recruiting experts at Tudor Collegiate Strategies. Find out more by visiting our website.

As a client, we can help you and your staff produce all of your recruiting messages, and organize them into a plan that maximizes you chances of success.

Dan Tudor can also bring his team to your school for one of our On-Campus Workshops. Contact us for the details.

If you have any questions, contact Dan Tudor or any of the Tudor Collegiate Strategies team by phone at 866.944.6732 or by e-mail at dan@dantudor.com.